Contents

Let's make music!

We can make music by banging!

Ravi **bangs** the drum.

Crash go the cymbals!

4

Making Music

Banging

Angela Aylmore

Heinemann

Little Nippers

H **www.heinemann.co.uk/library**
Visit our website to find out more information about **Heinemann Library** books.

To order:
☎ Phone 44 (0) 1865 888066
▤ Send a fax to 44 (0) 1865 314091
▢ Visit the Heinemann Bookshop at www.heinemann.co.uk/library to browse our catalogue and order online.

First published in Great Britain by Heinemann Library, Halley Court, Jordan Hill, Oxford OX2 8EJ, part of Harcourt Education.
Heinemann is a registered trademark of Harcourt Education Ltd.

Editorial: Kathy Peltan and Kate Bellamy
Design: Jo Hinton-Malivoire and Bigtop
Picture Research: Ruth Blair
Production: Severine Ribierre

Originated by Chroma Graphics (Overseas) Pte. Ltd
Printed and bound in China by South China Printing Company

ISBN 0 431 08821 7 (hardback)
10 09 08 07 06
10 9 8 7 6 5 4 3 2 1

ISBN 0 431 08826 8   (paperback)
09 08 07 06 05
10 9 8 7 6 5 4 3 2 1

British Library Cataloguing in Publication Data
Aylmore, Angela
Making Music: Banging
786.9
A full catalogue record for this book is available from the British Library.

Acknowledgements
The publishers would like to thank the following for permission to reproduce photographs: Alamy p. **15**; Corbis pp. **4b**, **5a**, **6**, **18**; Harcourt Education pp. **14** (Gareth Boden), **4a**, **5b** (Trevor Clifford), **13** (Peter Evans), **18** (Chris Honeywell), **7**, **8**, **9**, **10**, **11**, **12**, **16**, **17**, **19**, **20**, **21**, **22-23** (Tudor Photography).

Cover photograph of a girl playing a drum, reproduced with permission of Harcourt Education/Tudor Photography.

Every effort has been made to contact copyright holders of any material reproduced in this book. Any omissions will be rectified in subsequent printings if notice is given to the publishers.

The paper used to print this book comes from sustainable resources.

Tom hits his xylophone.

The triangle goes **ting ting**.

Tap it **gently**.
Keep it **soft**.

tap, tap, tap

Low and high

Let's play the glockenspiel.

Hit a low note.

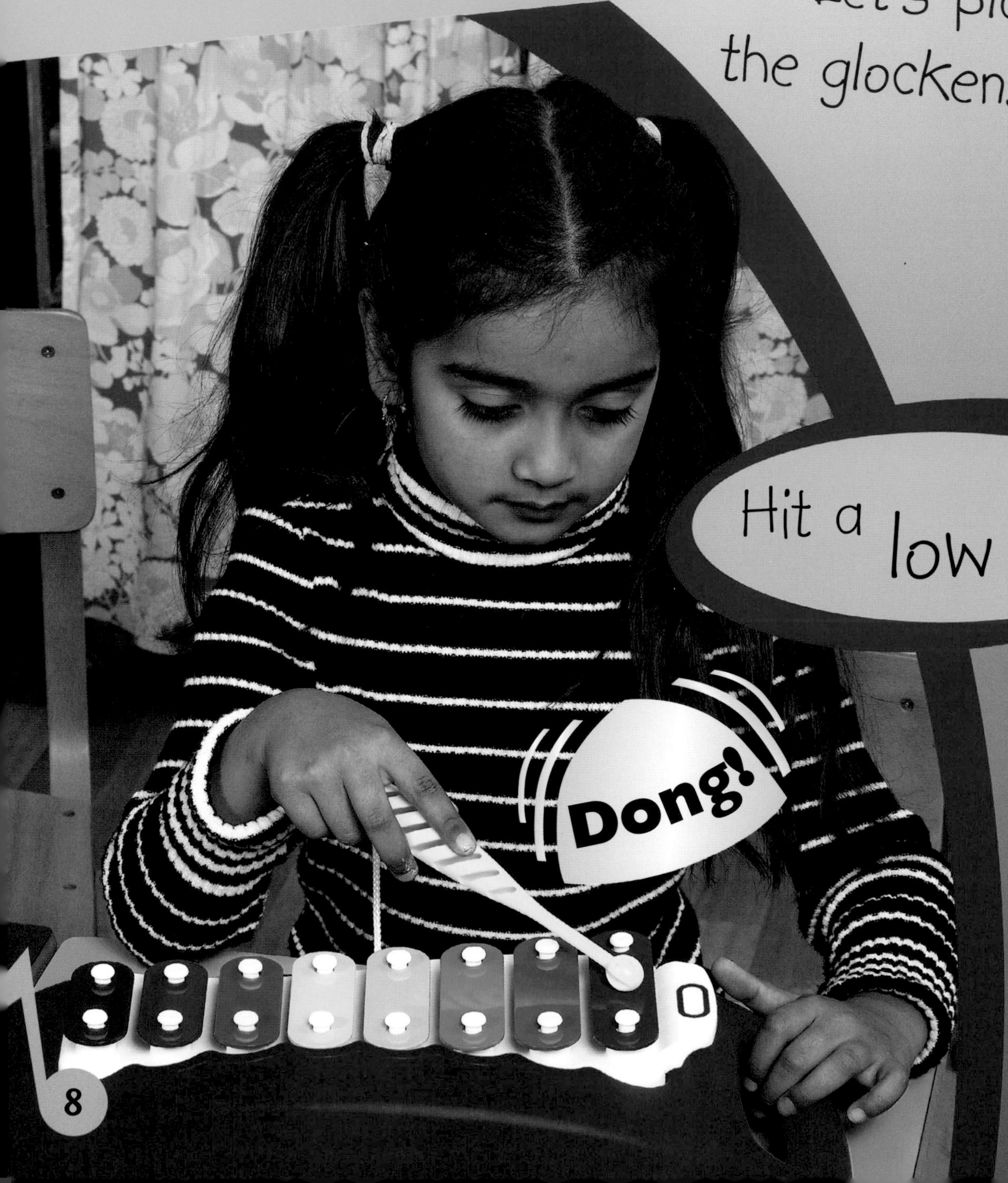

Make your own

Can you make a drum?

My drum is made from an old box.

Boom!

Can you play a pan?

Bang

Slow, slow. Faster and faster.

Sounds like...

clip-clop

What do the wooden blocks sound like?

Clip, clop,
clip, clop, like a
trotting horse!

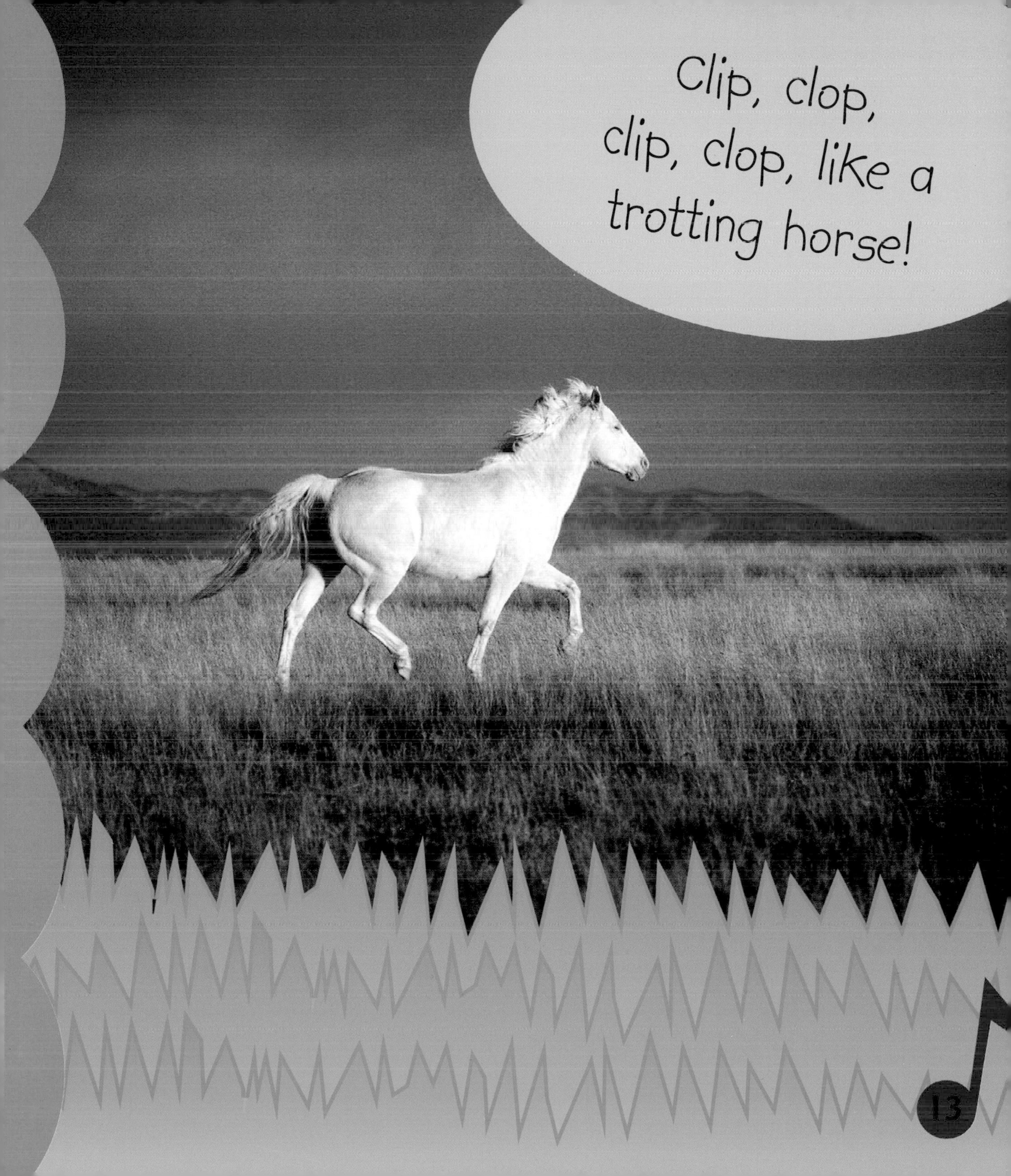

What are they?

These drums are from Indonesia.
They are called bonang.

A bonang sounds like a gong.

Play the cymbals

Bash the cymbals together!

Crash!

Tap them gently.

Ping

Keep in time

click-clack

castanets

The castanets click-clack.

The dancer's feet tip-tap.

tip-tap

Can you march
with the beat?

One, two.
One, two.

Listen carefully

What can you hear?

ting

triangle

maracas

violin

recorder

What makes that sound?

It's the triangle!